DIVING UNDER THE WAVES

by Andy Belcher

CAMBRIDGE
UNIVERSITY PRESS

UCL
Institute of Education

T0372617

UNDER THE SEA

About three quarters of the world's surface is covered by sea water, most of it in the great oceans. Some waters are very shallow, particularly near the coast. But some are very deep. Wonderful underwater landscapes can be seen in these deep waters. They have fascinating features for people to explore.

The Mariana Trench is the deepest part of the sea in the world. It reaches a depth of 10,994 metres - over 2,000 metres deeper than Mount Everest.

Mount Everest

Mariana Trench

There are amazing things under the sea like **coral reefs**, caves, **canyons**, **marine life**, shipwrecks and even treasure. There are still many things waiting to be discovered. People first started diving so they could visit this underwater. Now diving is a popular sport.

TYPES OF DIVING

There are several different ways of diving to explore the world underwater.

Freediving

In freediving, people dive and hold their breath. Until about 200 years ago, this was the only way for human beings to dive. Some people can hold their breath for several minutes. The problem is that most people can't dive for very long without having to come up to the surface to breathe.

FACT

New Zealander William Trubridge held his breath for a world record-breaking 4 minutes and 14 seconds and reached a depth of 102 metres.

Snorkelling

When snorkelling, people wear a face mask to see clearly, and a snorkel to breathe through. A snorkel is a type of tube which takes in air from above the water's surface. This is great for exploring shallow parts of the sea. However, the diver can only breathe at the sea surface, so can't stay underwater for very long, or dive down very deep.

Scuba diving

Scuba divers use an air tank and mask to keep breathing underwater. Then they can stay under for much longer and dive much deeper.

This diver has taken a deep breath through the snorkel and is swimming beneath the surface to have a close look at the coral.

DIVING IN THE PAST

Pearl diving

Pearls inside oyster shells were discovered many thousands of years ago. They became very valuable and many people like to wear them as jewellery.

Harvesting natural pearls first began in warm waters, such as in the Arabian Gulf. At first, free divers swam down to a depth of 1.5-2 metres to collect oysters with pearls inside. As pearls became more scarce, divers needed to swim down as deep as 40 metres to find the oysters. Freediving to such a depth was dangerous, as the divers couldn't come up to breathe often enough so could fall unconscious and drown.

This diver is tied to his boat so he can return to the surface easily. He has a basket around his neck to put the pearls in. ....

How a pearl is formed

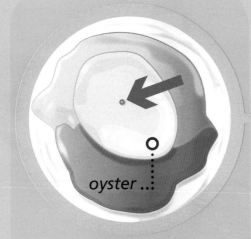

A grain of sand or grit enters the body of the oyster.

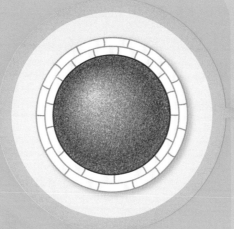

The oyster covers the grain of sand with special substance called nacre to protect itself.

After 2-3 years of coating the grain of sand with nacre, a pearl has formed.

Today, most pearls are farmed. Oyster farmers insert a small piece of shell into the oyster. The pearl takes two or three years to form.

Heavy diving suits

The diving suit was invented in the 18th century, to help people explore shipwrecks and recover **salvage**. In those days, lots of goods and money had to be transported by sailing boats, and many of these were sunk in storms or destroyed on rocks. Salvage hunters could become rich by recovering the goods or money from these wrecks.

This picture shows one of the first diving suits. Divers would be lowered into the water inside a heavy wooden tube with only their arms free.

By the 19th century, diving suits featured a heavy metal helmet. This fed air to the diver through a hose. The hose connected the helmet to air on the surface and was usually attached to a boat. The helmet was attached to a special **dry suit** with waterproof **seals**, which meant the diver stayed dry. The diver wore special clothing underneath the suit to stay warm. The suit was attached to heavy weighted boots so the diver would sink and be able to walk along the seabed.

However, this method meant that the divers weren't independent – they couldn't swim underwater and could only go as far or as deep as the length of the hose allowed.

This suit enabled divers to move more freely, but they could only walk, not swim.

The invention of Scuba diving

In 1943, Frenchmen Jacques Cousteau and
Emile Gagnan found a way to overcome this
challenge. They made a strong metal cylinder
and compressed a lot of air into it. It was strapped
onto the diver's back. They also made a regulator
with a hose and mouthpiece, which enabled
the diver to breathe from the tank. This new
invention was called SCUBA, which stands for ...

Jacques Cousteau

S Self **C** Contained **U** Underwater **B** Breathing **A** Apparatus

Jacques Cousteau diving
with three scuba tanks ...

GOING SCUBA DIVING

There are about 5 million people worldwide who scuba dive. Scuba diving can be dangerous, so divers need special equipment and proper training with an instructor.

The learner diver needs to wear the correct equipment. The **buoyancy** compensation device (BCD) is used to adjust how easy it is for the diver to float or sink during the dive.

glove

wet suit

dive bootie and fin

.... *mask and snorkle*

scuba tank with
regulator, gauges
.... *and BCD*

.... *weight belt*

Before they get into the water,
new divers need to learn how to dive
safely. An instructor teaches them how
to breathe with a scuba tank and use
a dive computer.

13

New divers usually start to learn how to dive in a swimming pool, so they can practise their new skills in clear, shallow water. To start with, they dive with a dive buddy. The dive buddy helps keep the new divers safe as they learn what to do.

In order to become fully qualified, new divers must complete two dives in either a lake or the sea. Then they are ready to go diving by themselves. However, they must still be very careful to keep an eye on the air gauge, and not go too deep, in case the air runs out. Divers must also be very careful when coming up from deep water to avoid getting the bends.

If a learner diver has any problems underwater, the buddy will be there to help.

THE BENDS

In deep water, water pressure is much greater, so the diver's body and the air inside it becomes compressed. If a diver comes up to the surface too quickly, the air in their body expands. This is called the bends. It is extremely painful and can be **fatal**. To prevent getting the bends, divers must breathe out regularly as they rise up to the surface.

OBSERVING MARINE LIFE

One of the amazing things about scuba diving is that a diver can observe marine life. There are over one million different types of animal living in the oceans across the world. Coral reefs are particularly interesting. They are home to thousands of fish and other animals. Although coral looks like beautiful pieces of rock or shell, it is made from tiny living creatures that live in **colonies**.

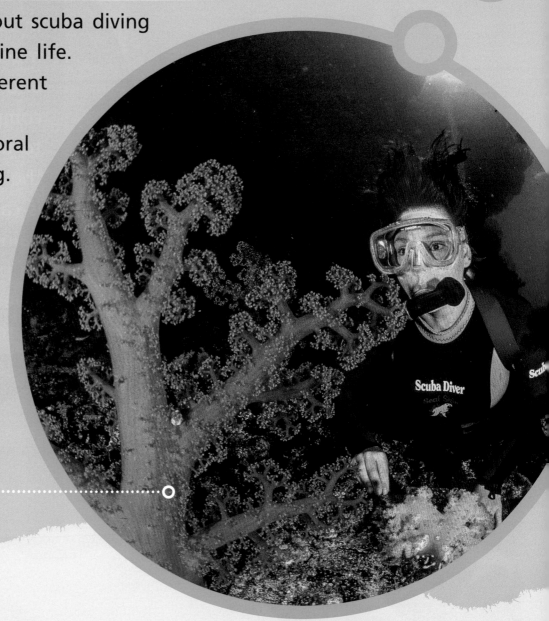

This diver is looking at a piece of orangey-brown coral.

It isn't always easy to observe marine life closely, as sea creatures are easily startled. Good divers are relaxed. They move slowly and carefully in order to get close to them.

Most marine creatures are safe to swim with – even enormous manta rays or whale sharks. Some animals, however, can be dangerous. Stone fish and lion fish lie camouflaged on the ocean floor. They are highly poisonous and if stepped on, the poison in their spines could kill a human.

Certain types of shark might attack and kill divers. The safest place to watch Great White Sharks is a Shark Safety cage.

The cage stops the shark getting to the diver. He can observe the shark from close up.

When the diver breathes out, the air tanks create bubbles in the water. These can scare the fish. This is why some divers use rebreathers. This type of tank recycles the **exhaled** air, rather than releasing it as bubbles. Rebreathers make it much easier for divers to get close to fish without causing distress. It is important to respect marine life and not to disturb it. For example, sea snakes are very poisonous but quite harmless if left alone.

Sometimes divers will photograph a new and rare species which no one has ever seen before. This helps extend people's knowledge of the ocean and it also makes an exciting news story.

Taking a photograph is the only way to see inside a giant clam. This photograph has helped scientists to study and understand how the body of a giant clam works.

This diver is using a rebreather so there are no bubbles. This means she has been able to get very close to this Grouper.

19

EXPLORING SHIPWRECKS

Shipwrecks happen for many different reasons. Some ships hit the shore and sink in shallow water. Others hit offshore reefs and sink slowly into deep water. Thousands of ships have been destroyed and sunk during wars. Many fighter planes and bombers were shot down, too.

Some wrecks lie in very deep water, but there are many in shallower waters which are safe for divers to explore. Wrecks which have been submerged for many years become home for a whole new **ecosystem** of marine life. Small animals can hide from predators in nooks and crannies, whilst different marine plants can grow on rusting metal or rotting wood.

FACT

In 1942, a huge American troop ship called the *SS President Coolidge* hit a **mine** near Vanuatu. The captain, Henry Nelson, ran it aground on a reef to stop it from sinking, and all 5340 men on board got safely ashore. The ship then slid down the reef with its **stern** lying in deep water. This is now a popular wreck for divers to visit because it is easy to get to and is full of interesting things.

This shipwreck is covered in marine plants, providing a home for many sea creatures.

Over time, wrecks become rusty and possibly unstable. Swimming in them can be dangerous. Exploring deep inside a big shipwreck requires special training. Divers have to be very careful not to get lost inside, as they have to return to the surface before air in their tanks runs out.

Some divers want to explore wrecks to see what they can salvage. Sometimes, shipwrecks may contain treasure, such as precious jewellery or even gold bars. The treasure may have been **stowed** in the hold, well away from the deck. This makes it dangerous to get to.

diver inside a shipwreck

EXTREME DIVING

Some forms of diving are more dangerous than others.

Ice Diving

In cold regions, like the Arctic, ice divers cut holes through ice to explore the seas beneath. Divers must be dressed in special **thermal** clothing underneath a dry suit, so they don't get cold in the freezing water. They use a powered digger to cut through ice which can be up to two metres thick. Whilst under the ice, divers remain attached to a safety line so they can easily find their way back to the hole. In such cold temperatures, the divers need to use special regulators with antifreeze so that their air supply doesn't freeze up.

safety line

23

Cavern and Cave Diving

Underwater caves are found in both saltwater oceans and freshwater lakes. Seawater caves can be astoundingly beautiful and full of fascinating marine life. But the dive can be dangerous. Deep freshwater cave divers may be underwater for several hours and cannot surface during that time. Such explorers will need special training to use ropes, lights and multiple tanks.

It is pitch black underground so good lighting is essential. Divers use powerful lights attached to their helmets and in their hands. Before the dive, all equipment needs to be carefully checked to see that everything is working correctly. As they enter the water, divers attach one end of their line to a solid object. They uncoil the line as they go further into the cave and then follow it back as they return. This is to prevent getting lost. Some caves are very narrow, so divers have to be careful not to get stuck.

a diver in an
underwater cave

WORKING UNDERWATER

How divers speak to each other

Divers cannot speak to each other when using a normal dive mask and regulator. Underwater documentary makers often equip their presenters with special masks which cover the whole face. The masks have a microphone inside so the diver can talk to other divers underwater and the boat crew on the surface. There is also a special ear speaker to hear the other divers.

built-in ear piece

built-in microphone

Going to even greater depths

A mini submarine offers a way to go much deeper underwater. It has its own air supply and so the divers do not need to wear diving gear. It has a clear glass dome port on the front so the divers inside can see everything under the water. The mini submarine enables the divers to encounter deep sea animals such as angler fish and brightly coloured sponges.

This mini submarine allows the divers to examine marine plants and coral.

DIVING AND CONSERVATION

Divers get close to some of the most beautiful marine life and ecosystems. However, they have a responsibility to be careful, and to respect the marine life around them.

Thanks to divers, much is now known about marine life. Scientists and marine biologists have been able to record the types and numbers of marine **species** under the sea. Using these records, scientists can see how pollution, global warming and the world's increasing population is affecting marine life.

Unfortunately, human activities are harming the oceans. Lots of plastic bags and toys end up in the sea. This plastic will stay there forever. Some marine animals die by getting tangled up in old abandoned fishing nets, or by eating plastic.

Sea temperatures are warming, and the ice caps of the Arctic and the Antarctic are melting. More and more fish are being fished from the sea. Waste from big cities and industry further **pollutes** the seas.

Divers may be able to help to solve these problems by using their records and observations to influence governments and media. New laws are needed to limit fishing and pollution. Television documentaries, books and websites can inform the public about the danger to marine life. Marine reserves, where marine life is better protected, provide places where divers can study the creatures, learning yet more about them.

The oceans and seas are fragile, but with the help of divers and explorers, they can be strengthened to protect sea creatures that live in them.

29

GLOSSARY

buoyancy   how something floats

canyons   very deep valleys

coral reefs   areas where coral is found

dry suit   diving clothing that keeps the diver dry

ecosystem   community of plants and animals that exist together

exhaled   breathed out

harvesting   collecting

marine life   creatures that can be found in the sea

pollutes   adds something to the water that shouldn't be there

predators   animals that hunt other animals

salvage   items rescued from a shipwreck

seals   closes securely to prevent water from entering

species   type of animal

stowed   put away

submersible   equipment that goes under the water

thermal   something able to keep someone or something warm

INDEX

Andy Belcher

The author, Andy Belcher, started diving in 1973. During his first dive trip to Papua New Guinea, Andy saw amazing colourful marine life and coral reefs. He became an underwater photographer so he could share these wonderful sights. Over the years, Andy has won over 80 photographic awards, including winning the British Wildlife Photographer of the Year Competition 1997.

Diving Under the Waves — Andy Belcher

Teaching notes written by Glen Franklin and Sue Bodman

Using this book

Content/theme/subject

In this non-fiction book, readers can discover how diving has developed from a human desire to see the world underwater to a popular sport and a form of exploration. Historical facts are combined with technical information, such as informing the reader about how divers can breathe underwater. There is an element of persuasion, considering the importance of conservation to preserve marine habitats, which is an appropriate level of challenge for Strand 2 readers.

Language structure

- Conventions for non-chronological report are followed, for example in the use of present tense: *'good lighting is essential'* (p.24) and generic subjects, such as *'divers'* and *'scientists'*.

- Sentences are longer and more complex, including embedded phrases (*'In cold regions, like the Arctic, divers cut holes ...'* on p.23) requiring careful reading for comprehension.

Book structure/visual features

- A logical structure is employed to take the reader through the development of diving techniques from early free-diving to the techniques of the present day.

- The book incorporates a range of text features, appropriate to the subject matter, including fact boxes to describe true-life historical events, and diagrams, such as to show how a pearl is formed (on p.7).

Vocabulary and comprehension

- Accurate technical vocabulary is used (*'snorkel'*, *'salvage'*, *'buoyancy'*), with the meaning supported by the context and by an extensive glossary.

- Emotive vocabulary, such as *'fragile'*, *'protect'*, *'responsibility'*, *'be careful'* is used on pp.28-29 to persuade the reader of the need for conservation.

Curriculum links

Science – There are many scientific experiments related to water and the sea. For example, children could explore salt water density: take two same size water jugs. Fill both with water. To one, add a large amount of salt. Now explore what happens when objects are lowered into the different jugs of water (eggs work particularly well for this experiment).

Art – Using the wonderful description of the marine worlds underwater, create a collage of a coral reef, including the different sorts of creatures that live there. Children may want to add a few divers and a shipwreck, too.

Learning outcomes

Children can:

- identify non-fiction text features, using these to aid comprehension

- summarise the main ideas from one or more paragraphs, using these to explain their understanding to others

- read complex sentences accurately, paying attention to punctuation and querying when the meaning is unclear.

Planning for guided reading

Lesson One: *Summarising the main ideas*

Ensure each child has a copy of the book. Ask them to read the title and the blurb quietly to themselves. Activate the group's prior knowledge by discussing what they know already about diving (this may vary greatly depending on the country and region where the children live). Establish that this is an information text, and review the non-fiction features, such as a glossary, index, fact boxes, diagrams, etc. Explain that non-fiction books are written for the reader to find out information. Say: *In this guided reading lesson, you are going to be exploring how to identify the main ideas and facts from this book about diving.*

Turn to p.2, and ask the children to read it quietly to themselves. Then demonstrate how you would pull out the main ideas from this page, noting down on a flipchart or whiteboard: *On this first page, the author is telling me that there is a lot of water around the world and some of it is very deep. He is also telling me that there are wonderful and interesting things to see underwater. So, if I wanted to summarise the key ideas on this page, I might write*